LIVING LIFE ON PURPOSE

A Blueprint For
Victorious Kingdom Living

YOLANDA R. MOSBY

LIVING LIFE ON PURPOSE

A Biblical Blueprint For Victorious Kingdom Living

All Rights Reserved.

Copyright © 2018 Yolanda R. Mosby

ISBN: 978-1-7329979-1-2

ALPHA BOOK PUBLISHING
4132 E. Joppa Rd. Suite 1123
Notthingham MD, 21236

TABLE OF CONTENTS

INTRODUCTION

It is hard to maintain peace during times of transition. Equally difficult is understanding the purpose of your life when you are experiencing brokenness from divorce, sickness, stressors, and defeats. However, finding your purpose is essential. It is a key element to enjoying your life.

The American Heritage Dictionary defines the word "purpose" as the object toward which one strives or for which something exists, an aim or goal. [1] If you believe you were created for a reason, and you are not on the earth to just exist (live), you will seek your purpose but may have a difficult time pinpointing what it is.

Unlike what many believe, your purpose is not to aspire to be a lawyer, farmer or talented guitarist. Rather, your purpose is to point you to your identity in Christ Jesus. In our materialistic world, many have set their affections on worldly pleasures and lived by earthly standards to determine their purposes. The trouble with this method is that many of us forget to plan for life's disappointments. Hence, the times of trouble break our spirits. These seasons of despair leave us broken. During those times, we

---

[1] www.pshychology/today.com

1

often hear, "God wants to put you back together again" but what does that mean and what does it look like?

Our solutions lie deep within our perception of ourselves and attitudes toward our circumstances. Therefore, it is important for you to begin an assessment of how you behave towards yourself. *"Neither give place to the devil"* (Ephesians 4:27 KJV). You know your identity when you rediscover your self-worth. Who you are becomes more recognizable when you line up with the will of God; your life truly is worth living.

Examine your relationship with God. Have you allowed doubt and fears to conqueror your thinking about how God views your life? We never want to imagine that we have lost hope. However, we should determine our outlook and stance towards our future. Things begin to fall into place when we include prayer and fasting in our lives. Our prayers, praise, and worship become personal, and we tune into God's plans for our lives on a daily basis. God really desires to restore you right in front of the very obstacles that challenge you the most.

CHAPTER 1

PREPARE TO SEE YOUR VISION COME TO PASS

As persons travel from one place to another, they must have an idea of how to arrive at their desired destination. In today's technologically charged world, many individuals utilize a Global Positioning System (GPS) to help them obtain directions and navigate to their chosen location. The GPS has become very popular and useful. It makes getting from one destination to the other easier by providing directions to the traveler who simply enters a starting and ending address into its system.

Similar to the GPS, God gives His people vision and direction. He provides specific instructions so they can move from their present positions to His desired purpose for their lives. "Vision" in the Hebrew, is derived from the word *chazown*, which means a "divine revelation that is also synonymous with a word from God through the means of prophecy, dreams, and visions." [2]

God can reveal His vision for your life in various ways.

---

[2] https://www.blueletterbible.org/lang/lexicon/lexicon.cfm?Strongs=H2377&t=KJV

Take a moment to capture how the vision of your life can be unveiled.

Commune with God and Receive a Word

To clearly understand God's vision for your life, you must be able to identify His voice and stand firm on His Word. At times, you may become fearful because you are in an unfamiliar situation or facing unusual circumstances. However, you should resist the temptation to deviate from the Word. Your vision will come in the form of instructions or directions—sometimes both. The directions will include a starting and ending point, while the instructions will entail detailed information on how it will be done.

In Genesis 12:1-3, God spoke a word to Abram and gave him a vision for his family and future descendants:

> *Now the Lord had said unto Abram, Get thee out of thy country, and from thy kindred, and from thy father's house, unto a land that I will shew thee: And I will make of thee a great nation, and I will bless thee, and make thy name great; and thou shalt be a blessing: And I will bless them that bless thee, and curse him that curseth thee: and in thee shall all families of the earth be blessed" (KJV).*

God's vision for Abram included his departure from his home country into a new land. God also gave him an affirmation that He would enlarge Abram and his offspring. Furthermore, God promised to prosper those who bless Abram's seed and afflict those who would curse them.

Expect a Holy Visitation

When God reveals His vision to someone, he/she becomes the "visionary" – the one whom God entrusts to bring about His vision. Often times, we start with a word and wait for the revelation of the word. God is telling you to get back to writing down the vision because He will visit you when you obey. When God sent the angel to speak to Mary, he said:

> *"Thou shalt conceive in thy womb and bring forth a son and shalt call his name JESUS…He shall be great and would be called the Son of the Highest: and the Lord God shall give unto him the throne of his father David: And he shall reign over the house of Jacob forever; and of his Kingdom there shall be no end" (Luke 1:31-33 KJV).*

Luke the physician asserts that through the voice of the angel, God revealed unto Mary the vision for her Son's life. He told her what His name would be, that He would be great, those He would rule over, and how long He would rule.

Create Writing Prompted by the Holy Spirit

Vision is "God-inspired, a cooperative venture with Him and a compelling picture of a better future that inspires people to become involved and contribute to the common good."[3] To perceive vision, you must continually commune with God in prayer. As you continue to

---

[3] Vision and Mission, Regent School of Divinity, Spiritual Formation Lecture, Dr. Joseph Flynn, 2012

fellowship with God, He will reveal to you how He sees your life; that is the vision. The key to developing that vision is to perceive what God sees.

God instructed the prophet Habakkuk to *"Write the vision and make it plain upon tables that he may run that readeth it"* (Habakkuk 2:2 KJV). In other words, the vision is developed through writing. Writing expresses the vision. It informs and persuades the reader. The vision must be communicated by the visionary and read continually by others who will help bring it to fruition. Reading the vision aloud daily keeps you focused on what God has said about who you are and what He has called you to do. When you understand the purpose of the vision and the benefits you will yield, you can execute it appropriately, as well as contribute the necessary resources to help the vision become a reality.[4]

Developing a clear and concise vision is crucial. You must start with the end in mind and visualize what you ultimately want to become. "It is not enough, however, to be able to visualize (and write the vision). When you only have a vision you are primarily a dreamer. Unfortunately, visions cannot just be plucked out of thin air and made into a reality. You must map out the necessary steps that you intend to take to arrive at the vision in mind. Set short, medium, and long-term goals for yourself, business, organization or ministry. Thereafter, review

---

[4] Casting the Vision, Christians Equipping Christians for Outreach Fellowship Workshop. Dr. Nadie DuBose. November 13-14, 2009

them periodically" [5] and document when they have been achieved.

Igniting Your Vision

1. Pray to God (Philippians 4:6-8)

2. Believe that God has answered your prayer (Mark 11:22-24)

3. Ask the Holy Spirit to lead you to a scripture to meditate on (John 16:13)

4. Meditate – allow the Holy Spirit to give you understanding (Psalm 1:2)

5. Put the Word into action by asking the Holy Spirit where to go and who to speak with (Proverbs 3:5-6)

6. Do exactly what He says regarding where to go and who to speak with (John 2:5)

7. Continually thank God for what He has done (Ephesians 5:20; 1 Thessalonians 5:18) [6]

---

[5] Dr. Clifton R. Clarke. Called to Serve. 2007. STEP Publishers. Accra, Ghana.

[6] Helping the Vision Come About. Personal Blog. Dr. Nadie DuBose. November 4, 2007.

NOTES

NOTES

CHAPTER 2

DISCOVERING GOD'S BLUEPRINT

Digging beneath the surface can be hard work, but it reaps great benefits. You will discover your purpose in life. God has created individualized plans that are designed to propel you through every season. If you take a closer look at the job of an architect, you will get a better understanding of God's blueprints. The word "blueprint" originated to provide the accurate reproduction of specific designs used in construction. [7] When God constructed your life, He also created a blueprint to reproduce ways the power of the Holy Spirit can be in full operation on the earth. Your path in life has been designed by the master architect—Jesus Christ. His layout and plans for you include specific details of your life from the day of conception to the day you rest in the grave.

Every trial and tribulation has been carefully planned. This includes our mishaps, setbacks, triumphs, and victories. God's layouts and plans for your life are based on the Jeremiah 29:11 decree: *"For I know the thoughts that I*

---

[7] www.merriam-webster.com

think toward you, saith the Lord, thoughts of peace, and not of evil, to give you an expected end"(KJV). As a believer with a purposed life, you should have confidence in knowing God's blueprint for your life.

Here are two practical steps that will give you confidence in God's blueprint for maximizing your time and living on purpose.

Align Your Thoughts with God's Thoughts about You

Take the time to examine yourself daily so you can identify the areas of procrastination or sins that can cause a detour from God's plans. He has great expectations that you will work to build His kingdom. Never compromise your destiny and mission with the spirit of sabotage, negative thoughts or vain imaginations. Be excited about God's plans and what He has designed for the rest of your life. Refuse to let regrets, condemnation or guilt settle in and hinder you from walking in your best days. *"For my thoughts are not your thoughts, neither are your ways my ways, saith the LORD"* (Isaiah 55:8 KJV).

At times, situations may look worse than they appear. You may even feel as if the problems in your life are getting worse instead of better. "Before deliverance, things will deteriorate for a greater victory. Your doubts must cease. You must wait in faith and align your expectations with what the word says."[8]

---

[8] www.JamesMcDonald.com

Understand that Everyone Has an Expected End

God expects the work He has ordained for your life to be completed prior to your expected end. Beyond a shadow of a doubt, your days upon the earth are the best ones to further the gospel and demonstrate greater works. *"For surely there is an end; and thine expectation shall not be cut off"* (Proverbs 23:18 KJV). Every morning you awake from your sleep is a new beginning let God use you for His glory. In sickness or pain, trial or tribulation, you must trust God's blueprint. *"Being confident of this very thing, that he which hath begun a good work in you will perform it until the day of Jesus Christ"* (Philippians 1:6 KJV). God has already declared your end from the very beginning.

"There are times when God calls us to work or times he will require us to rest. Despite which state you may be in, please know that God continues to work while we are resting."[9] Therefore, you must persistently submit yourself to Him until He calls you home to glory. He is your Teacher and High Priest. When you become weary in well doing, it means you are in a season of unbelief. However, God wants you to receive a word in this season that will motivate you to work until He calls you into divine rest. He will continue to lead you through feelings of incompleteness. You must actively pursue righteousness through God's faithfulness and love. Learn of Christ and cease from your thoughts and labor.

---

[9] Barnett, Virginia sermon "Divine Rest" July 9, 2017

How to Disclose the Blueprint for Your Life

1. Clear your mind of distractions that could clutter your thinking process

2. Ask God to reveal your direction (start and end points)

3. Take a mental and written note of every detailed instruction by journaling

4. Design solutions to maximize your achievements even during the toughest circumstances

5. Intentionally interact with God, as well as spiritual advisors who can give godly counsel and confirm God's plan for your life

NOTES

NOTES

CHAPTER 3

KNOW WHO AND WHOSE YOU ARE

"To live is to choose, but to choose well, you must know who you are and what you stand for, where you want to go and why you want to go there."[10]

Your identity describes who you are. In our earthly affairs, a driver's license, passport or social security card is necessary to verify a person's identity. Whenever you travel out of town or to another country, identification must be presented and verified before you can go through customs. Moreover, if a person walks into a bank to withdraw funds from an account, the teller will request some form of identification to ensure that the funds are being paid to the rightful owner.

"But ye are a chosen generation, a royal priesthood, an holy nation, a peculiar people; that ye should shew forth the praises of him who hath called you out of darkness into his marvelous light" (1 Peter 2:9 KJV).

We Are the People of God!

You are called out of darkness into the family of royalty. God has advocated for your life and paid for it with the ultimate sacrifice. Therefore, your identity is not defined by society or your past sins. Although you have sinned, God's mercy will continue to bestow a bounty of blessings upon your life when you repent and turn away from sin. *"Which in time past were not a people, but are now the people of God; which had not obtained mercy, but are now the people of God; which had not obtained mercy, but now have obtained mercy"* (1 Peter 2:10 KJV).

We Are Royal People!

Being royal is being a part of God's kingdom. You are kingdom minded and kingdom influenced. *"And if children, then heirs; heirs of God, and joint-heirs with Christ; if so be that we suffer with him, that we may be also glorified together"* (Romans 8:17 KJV). Who we are, which is our spiritual identity, is also verified by spiritual leaders and other believers who take the time to help us mature in our relationship with Christ.

A seed of faith is conceived in your spirit when you first accept Christ as your personal Savior. Thereafter, the seed begins to grow as you receive nurturing through the Word of God. Your royal identity is unveiled when you consistently worship, study God's Word, and fellowship with other believers. It is also important to incorporate a relationship with spiritual mentors. These foundational building blocks will help you to understand what it means to have accepted your royal identity.

We Are a Peculiar People!

God is waiting for His sons and daughters to be revealed to the earth. *"For the earnest expectation of the creature waiteth for the manifestation of the sons of God"* (Romans 8:19 KJV). Let's face it, you are an unusual individual. You are unique. Hence, you should reject every plan that tries to fit you perfectly into the world. Sanctification by the Holy Spirit spiritually separates you from the world and dedicates you to God for His purpose. In addition, you are commissioned by the Holy Spirit to accomplish a specific task for God. As a result, you start to understand who God has called you to be and the purpose He has predestined you to fulfill on the earth. After you receive instructions from God about who you are, He will fill you with the Holy Spirit. Consequently, you can activate your call and God-given purpose to a make a difference in the world.

You demonstrate whose you are by your relationship with God and a willingness to be led by His Spirit. The Holy Scriptures declares, *"So God created man in his own image, in the image of God created he him; male and female created he them"* (Genesis 1:27KJV). The word "created" is derived from the Hebrew word *bara*, which means to form and shape. The word "image" is derived from the Hebrew word *tselem*, which means resemblance and likeness. Therefore, the children of God are formed and shaped into God's likeness to reflect His nature (His love) for others. "You don't put an image of somebody up and hope nobody notices it… without making any connection between the image and reality. You are in the image of God in order to display God, to show God, that's what you're about. That's your meaning. That's your identity."[11]

Most importantly, your identity must be founded in your personal relationship with Christ and the Holy Scriptures, not church, ministry or other people's opinions. To truly know yourself, you must understand God. More importantly, your identity is also found in how you perceive yourself. *"For as he thinketh in his heart, so is he; eat and drink, saith he to thee, but his heart is not with thee"* (Proverbs 23:7 KJV). Evidently, how you see yourself determines who you will be. Therefore, you should think of yourself as God thinks of you. It is impossible for you to know yourself outside of God. His plan is a direct revelation of who you really are.[12]

Discover Your Who

1. Establishing healthy mentoring relationships with spiritual leaders will serve as a guide (1 Timothy 1:1-2)

2. Maintain a healthy and consistent relationship with God (Jude 1:20)

---

[11] Identity and Desire.
https://l.facebook.com/l.php?u=https%3A%2F%2Fwww.desiringgod.org%2Fmessages%2Fidentity-and-desire&h=AT2OhpZbBNqIYCKIvQ7STOG4ERiT-r5_zVo32K6lqbAvd9is2HO7nZ-XpH3x7ay84ifI3ecL-fin12eWNqVawkHt8Zbynwvjo_BdmWHufhoMFTmWiM9no3iPB8_zxT-vQw

[12] Pastoral Theology. The Minister's Marriage and Family Life: Ministerial Identity. Dr. James Flynn. November 28, 2014.

3. Reexamine your level of commitment unto the Lord (Matthew 22:37)

4. Commune with God in prayer and be filled with the Holy Spirit daily (Acts 2:3-4)

NOTES

NOTES

CHAPTER 4

THE ATTITUDE OF GRATITUDE AND BOLDNESS

Maintain an appreciation for living life on purpose. Start your mornings off thanking God for a purposeful and meaningful life that is filled with His promises. Make it a practice to express your gratitude to the Father on a regular basis. *"So I will sing praise unto thy name for ever, that I may daily perform my vows"* (Psalm 61:8 KJV).

If you choose to face your daily task without spending time in meditation and prayer, it will be very challenging. However, giving God a portion of your day, which means giving Him the first fruits of your day by rising early for prayer will make life easier.

Have an appreciation for the gifts God has instilled within you by controlling your habits, thoughts, and behaviors. You can accomplish this through discipline and a spirit of gratitude. Your relentless devotion to God lets you obtain every good thing He has designed. Respond to God before, during, and after prayer with thanksgiving as an expression of your gratitude. God has been faithful to you, so you should bless His holy name.

Don't let men spoil you with vain imaginations. Reject the desire to obtain all the praise for your successes. God's Word rooted within you will build you up and cause you to achieve; therefore, it deserves all the recognition. Your gratitude will promote a new direction that will be revealed during prayer. Gratitude also causes your trials and tribulations to come to a perfected end. Practicing being thankful inspires you to look forward to new beginnings, experiences, and encounters with the Father.

If you cultivate an atmosphere of reverence, you can obtain the king's favor. *" For thou, Lord, wilt bless the righteous; with favour wilt thou compass him as with a shield"* (Psalms 5:12 KJV). Overthinking a situation can get you stuck. In fact, being overly analytical can stunt your growth and prevent you from progressing in life. The best strategy is to synchronize your thoughts with God's. That will shift the atmosphere and remove the fear that has crippled you. Believe that God will do for you what you have never witnessed. Move from the "not enough" to "more than enough" phase in your life. Don't become vulnerable to the Enemy's attacks. Stand up in boldness against the strongman. Repossess everything the Devil has stolen from you. *"In whom we have boldness and access with confidence by the faith of him"* (Ephesians 3:12 KJV).

Prayer for Revelation and Knowledge

For this cause I bow my knees unto the Father of our Lord Jesus Christ, of whom the whole family in heaven and earth is named, That he would grant you, according to the riches of his glory, to be strengthened with might by His Spirit in the inner man, that Christ may dwell in your hearts by faith; that ye being rooted and grounded in love, may be able to comprehend with all saints what is the breadth, and length, and depth, and height. And to know the love of Christ, which passeth knowledge, that ye might be filled with all the fullness of God. Now unto him that is able to do exceeding abundantly above all that we ask or think, according to the power that worketh in us. Unto him be glory in the church by Christ Jesus throughout all ages, world without end. Amen (Ephesians 3:14-21 KJV).

How to Walk in Boldness

- Offer praise to God for accepting you into the family

- Believe that God has redeemed you through the blood of His Son Jesus Christ, and has forgiven your sins according to the riches of his grace

- Allow the mysteries to be made known unto you according to His good pleasure, which He hath purposed

- Believe that God has granted you boldness and total access by faith

NOTES

NOTES

CHAPTER 5

THE GIFT OF SALVATION

God has given every individual a gift. You can access the free gift of salvation with your heart and confessions of faith. God has a strong desire for you to live, not only here on earth but also eternally in heaven. However, everlasting life is only available to those who have personally accepted Jesus Christ as their Lord and Savior. *"For God so loved the world that he gave his only begotten Son, that whosoever believeth in him should not perish, but have everlasting life"* (John 3:16 KJV). The unveiling gift of salvation gives each of us the opportunity to live with purpose. God's love that He has showered upon you will thrust you into the next season of harvest.

He Gave His Only Begotten Son

Many want to believe our salvation was free; however, the Bible tells us a costly price was paid. *"And whosoever doth not bear his cross, and come after me, cannot be my disciple"* (Luke 14:27 KJV). It doesn't matter what your past sins were. "To us it's free, but it cost God the life of His Son. The reason is that on the cross Jesus Christ became the final sacrifice for our sins. He paid for our salvation with his blood."[13] How will you respond to this free gift? Your response is to receive Him wholeheartedly. He will not force the gift upon you. Rather, God wants to restore your life. He specializes in putting crushed and bruised spirits back together again. No matter if cancer or divorce has come as Goliaths in your life, He will give you the stone to conquer your enemy.

You need to follow the biblical framework of countless men and women who have defined their purpose in God. Familiarize yourself with Bible stories. They serve as comfort and reassurance of the great work God is able to do in your life. Without the testimonies of the saints, we would struggle with our faith.

Whosoever Believeth in Him Should Not Perish but Have Everlasting Life

Once you accept Jesus into your life, He makes you a new living creature; the old things have passed away. *"That if thou shalt confess with thy mouth the Lord Jesus, and believe in thine heart that God hath raised him from the dead, thou shalt be saved"* (Romans 10:9 KJV). Every lash Jesus bore on His back was for the living. Many may not understand that everlasting life is for those who believe.

Unbelief and doubt cause you to perish. They cause the inner man to perish. Your vision and dreams perish along with your desire to live on purpose. You must speak life

---

[13] www.BillyGraham.org (2015)

over yourself. Don't just speak inwardly but shout it out! *"I shall not die, but live, and declare the works of the LORD"* (Psalm 118:17 KJV). Remind yourself of the promise over and over and over again until it sinks deep into your soul. Write declarations and affirmations over your life on purpose. You cannot wait until sickness and disease overtake your body to speak life. Start right now! Affirm your faith today. Refuse to bow down to strange voices; instead, follow the leading of the good Shepherd.

Speak it out! Make Affirmations

1. I have a new purpose for living

2. My body, soul, and spirit, will synchronize with my life's purpose

3. Each day, I will seek God for precise instructions for living my best life

4. I will obtain greater faith to walk in the power of the risen Savior

5. I will not be discouraged; instead, I will inspire myself and others to live on purpose

NOTES

NOTES

CHAPTER 6

START LIVING YOUR BEST LIFE ON PURPOSE

Rick Warren wrote one of the most memorable best sellers called *The Purposed Driven Life: What on Earth am I here for?* The success of this book neither stemmed from the author's popularity nor the endorsements but the answers to basic life questions. Everyone wants to know the answers to "Why am I here and what is my purpose?" After God reveals the answers to your questions, it is time to live your best life on purpose. It's time to steam straight ahead *"Because strait is the gate, and narrow is the way, which leadeth unto life, and few there be that find it"* (Matthew 7:14 KJV). God is on your side in spite of how dismal your path may be. Sometimes, you have to travel the rough road, but He will lead you through the right gate. "Time is your most precious gift because you only have a set amount of it. You can make more money, but you can't make more time. When you give someone your time, you are giving them a portion of your life that you'll never get back."[14]

---

[14] Warren, Richard (1954) The Purpose Driven Life: What on Earth am I here

Do everything in your power not to yield to temptation. In fact, as Scripture teaches, shun the very appearance of evil (See 1Thessalonians 5:22). Take your place as a watchman on the walls looking for your adversary.

Prayer is the master key to defeating the Enemy. Every believer is called to prayer. Sometimes we don't know who or what to pray for but the Spirit always helps us by making intercession for us.[15] He will give you godly hints to know what to do, where to go, and what to say. You can reach the highest mountain or cross the deepest sea when you choose to live your best life on purpose.

Give God your best gifts, and He will give you His finest. Coveting what others have or comparing yourself to them can be very dangerous. It can also imply that you have taken your eyes off of God. When your eyes are not focused on the Master, you are giving Him secondhand attention, which is not your best. Scripture specifically states, *"But covet earnestly the best gifts; and yet shew I unto you a more excellent way"* (1 Corinthians 12:31 KJV). In this scriptural text, the apostle Paul teaches how to covet in a godly way. If you want to set your affections on people, make sure they are those who utilize their gifts to the best of their abilities. You should desire the best gifts of prophesying, teaching, performing miracles, healing diseases, speaking, and interpreting tongues.[16] *"Though I speak with tongues of men and of angels, and have not charity, I am*

---

for? Grand Rapids, Mich. Zondervan, 2002
[15] Romans 8:26 KJV
[16] www.biblestudytools.com

become as sounding brass, or a tinkling cymbal. And though I have the gift of prophecy, and understand all mysteries, and all knowledge; and though I have faith, so that I could remove mountains, and have not charity, I am nothing" (1 Corinthians 13:1-2 KJV).

Don't just observe those who operate in gifts but fervently seek to serve God in a more useful and productive way. Your observations will not only show strategies to use, but they will also show specific techniques to drive you forward. Be zealous for the Lord and intentional about living your best life.

Best Practices for Living on Purpose

1. Improve your time and self-management skills

2. Remain focused on God

3. Hold yourself accountable for mistakes and learn from them

4. Seek clarity on how you can continue to grow and serve the Lord

NOTES

NOTES

CONCLUSION

The time has come for you not to just live but to live on purpose. If you want a better life, start with a healthier you. You must take time to speak over your life and fill your atmosphere with words that promote healing. You have the power of God inside you. Satan cannot and will not defeat you. Through prayer, you can obtain the keys to access a greater life. Restoration is a process that takes time and lots of patience. *"Knowing this, that the trying of your faith worketh patience"* (James 1:3 KJV).

Your life can be restored to the original design God created from the beginning. You will be strengthened when you are sick. You will be healed when you have diseases. You will be mended when you are broken. Those who have scattered will be brought back. Those who are lost will be found. You have a spiritual responsibility let God be in total control of your life. Your attitude should reflect your perception of who God is. You must truly appreciate the plan God has created for you.

Maintain a spirit of expectancy that your life's plan will be accomplished. Take time to discover your purpose, which will lead to your assignment. Remember, the assignment can only be fulfilled with a vision and following God's blueprints. Your life is more important than your job description, marital status or mother and fatherhood. There is more to life than taking a vacation and planning holiday parties.

NOTES

NOTES

www.ingramcontent.com/pod-product-compliance
Lightning Source LLC
Chambersburg PA
CBHW071117090426
42736CB00029B/2678